PRAYERS
FOR CHILDREN

PRAYERS
FOR CHILDREN

ILLUSTRATED BY
RACHEL TAFT DIXON

SIMON AND SCHUSTER · NEW YORK

THE LITTLE GOLDEN BOOKS ARE PREPARED UNDER THE SUPERVISION OF
MARY REED, PH.D.
FORMERLY OF TEACHERS COLLEGE, COLUMBIA UNIVERSITY

About the Artist

RACHEL TAFT DIXON has taught at the Pratt Institute and Hartford Art School, designed children's clothes, and illustrated many children's books and magazine stories.

 DESIGNED AND PRODUCED BY THE SANDPIPER PRESS AND ARTISTS AND WRITERS GUILD, INC. PRINTED IN THE U.S.A. BY WESTERN PRINTING AND LITHOGRAPHING COMPANY
PUBLISHED BY SIMON AND SCHUSTER, INC., ROCKEFELLER CENTER, NEW YORK 20, NEW YORK

Father, We Thank Thee

For flowers that bloom about our feet,
  Father, we thank Thee,
For tender grass so fresh and sweet,
  Father, we thank Thee,
For the song of bird and hum of bee,
For all things fair we hear or see,
Father in heaven, we thank Thee.

For blue of stream and blue of sky,
  Father, we thank Thee,
For pleasant shade of branches high,
  Father, we thank Thee,
For fragrant air and cooling breeze,
For beauty of the blooming trees,
Father in heaven, we thank Thee.

For this new morning with its light,
  Father, we thank Thee,
For rest and shelter of the night,
  Father, we thank Thee,
For health and food, for love and friends,
For everything Thy goodness sends,
Father in heaven, we thank Thee.

—Ralph Waldo Emerson

For flowers that bloom about our feet,
Father, we thank Thee.

For tender grass so fresh and sweet,
Father, we thank Thee.

The Lord's Prayer

Our Father, who art in heaven, Hallowed be Thy Name.

Thy kingdom come, Thy will be done in earth as it is in heaven.

Give us this day our daily bread, and forgive us our debts, as we forgive our debtors.

And lead us not into temptation, but deliver us from evil.

For thine is the kingdom, and the power, and the glory, for ever.

Amen.

R.T.D.

For the song of bird and hum of bee,
Father in heaven, we thank Thee.

Dear Father, Hear and Bless

Dear Father, hear and bless
Thy beasts and singing birds:
And guard with tenderness
Small things that have no words.

A Great Gray Elephant

A great gray elephant,
A little yellow bee,
A tiny purple violet,
    A tall green tree,

A red and white sailboat
On a blue sea—
All these things
You gave to me,
When you made
My eyes to see—
Thank you, God!

Reprinted by permission of
The National Society for the
Prevention of Blindness, Inc.

For all things fair we hear or see,
Father in heaven, we thank Thee.

Good-night Prayer

Father, unto Thee I pray,
Thou hast guarded me all day;
Safe I am while in Thy sight,
Safely let me sleep tonight.

Bless my friends, the whole world bless;
Help me to learn helpfulness;
Keep me ever in Thy sight;
So to all I say good night.

—Henry Johnstone

America

Our Fathers' God, to Thee,
Author of liberty,
To Thee we sing.
Long may our land be bright
With freedom's holy light;
Protect us by Thy might,
Great God, our King.

—Samuel Francis Smith

He Prayeth Well, Who Loveth Well

He prayeth well, who loveth well
Both man and bird and beast.

He prayeth best, who loveth best
All things both great and small;
For the dear God who loveth us,
He made and loveth all.

—*Samuel Taylor Coleridge,*
from *The Ancient Mariner*

Jesus, Tender Shepherd, Hear Me

Jesus, tender Shepherd, hear me;
  Bless Thy little lamb tonight;
Through the darkness be Thou near me,
  Watch my sleep till morning light.

All this day Thy hand has led me,
  And I thank Thee for Thy care;
Thou has warmed and clothed and fed me;
  Listen to my evening prayer.

—*Mary L. Duncan*

The Twenty-third Psalm

The Lord is my shepherd; I shall not want.
He maketh me to lie down in green pastures: He leadeth me beside the still waters.
He restoreth my soul: He leadeth me in the paths of righteousness for His name's sake.
Yea, though I walk through the valley of the shadow of death, I will fear no evil: for Thou art with me; Thy rod and Thy staff, they comfort me.
Thou preparest a table before me in the presence of mine enemies. Thou anointest my head with oil; my cup runneth over.
Surely goodness and mercy shall follow me all the days of my life: and I will dwell in the house of the Lord for ever.

For fragrant air and cooling breeze,
Father in heaven, we thank Thee.

I Thank Thee, Lord, for Quiet Rest

I thank Thee, Lord, for quiet rest,
And for Thy care of me;
O let me through this day be blest
And kept from harm by Thee.

—Mary L. Duncan

For this new morning with its light,
Father, we thank Thee.

Thank You, God

God made the sun
 And God made the tree,
God made the mountains
 And God made me.

I thank you, O God,
 For the sun and the tree,
For making the mountains
 And for making me.

—Leah Gale

Bedtime Prayer

Now I lay me down to sleep;
I pray Thee, Lord, my soul to keep.
If I should die before I wake,
I pray Thee, Lord, my soul to take.

For rest and shelter of the night,
Father, we thank Thee.

A Child's Grace

Thank you for the world so sweet,
Thank you for the food we eat,
Thank you for the birds that sing—
Thank you, God, for everything.

—Mrs. E. R. Leatham

R.T.D.

Grace

Be present at our table, Lord;
Be here and everywhere adored.
Thy creatures bless, and grant that we
May feast in paradise with Thee.

—John Wesley

For health and food, for love and friends,
Father, we thank Thee.

The Doxology

Praise God, from whom all blessings flow;
Praise Him, all creatures here below;
Praise Him above, ye heavenly host:
Praise Father, Son, and Holy Ghost. Amen.

For everything Thy goodness sends,
Father in heaven, we thank Thee.

Jesus, from Thy Throne on High

(Litany)

Jesus, from Thy throne on high,
  Far above the bright blue sky,
Look on me with loving eye;
  Hear me, Holy Jesus.

Be Thou with me every day,
  In my work and in my play,
When I learn and when I pray;
  Hear me, Holy Jesus.

—*Thomas B. Pollock*

Good Night

Good night! Good night!
Far flies the light;
But still God's love

Shall flame above,
Making all bright.
Good night! Good night!

The Four Freedoms

God keep this country free:
Free from tyrants and their whips
To stamp out truth and seal the lips;
Free for every race and creed,
Free from fear,
Free from need;
God keep this country free.

—*Leah Gale*

Index

P